Praise

Reader beware. This book of poetry will hold you captive. E.J. Rode dares to write that "Love is always a miracle—no matter how it ends." She speaks of unbearable loss. "Growing old was something—we'd do—together." "Didn't you know—that you were the story—I always wanted to hear." She remembers, ". . .my hand against your skin—never wishing I'd touched you less." She faces despair and cries out, ". . .over and over again I find myself lost." "Even the truth has learned to lie." Repeatedly, she returns to the moon for solace, a moon that is "always too much, and never enough." She ". . .silently scolds the clock for ticking." She declares, ". . .of my failings I can only tell—I've fallen short—but loved so well." She abides by her advice: "Write poems you fear no one will like. . ." Truth at all cost. Expect nothing else from this poet. *No Matter How It Ends* is a masterpiece by a highly skilled poet who dares to live life on her own terms.

> —Marcel Aimé Duclos, author of *Unavoidable . . .evade dying at your own peril* (Black Forest Publishing, 2021)

We're fortunate that Meadowlark Press has invited poet E.J. Rode to share her powerful, private conversations with us in this collection, *No Matter How It Ends*. It's quite an undertaking, but E.J. has followed her own advice: "Write the poems you fear no one else will like."

E.J., and her poems, are exceptional. She's a talented writer whose literary work is creative, observant, elegant, honest, and inspiring. She pays attention to the smallest sensory detail. I feel like, if at any moment I were to ask her, "Right now, where is the moon in the sky?" she'd accurately describe its location, shape, and its effect on her mood.

Thanks to E.J.'s masterful poetry, I'm less judgmental, think more deeply, and better understand our world and myself.

If there were a position of Poet of Peace, and if I were in charge, I'd appoint E.J. With her literary wisdom, openness, and loving connection with humanity, there could be resolution to many of life's issues and personal problems.

—Jim Potter, author of *Deputy Jennings Meets the Amish*

*Love is always a miracle
no matter how it ends*

. . .

*We've forever hungered for
how sweet at last to savor*

*with no cast shadow
of what will come*

. . .

We sense immediately that this marvelous collection of poetry will be like no other. If we have thought to live more fully, to reach deeper, to pull more from life, then this is the directive, the encyclical.

The abiding thesis is simple—the immense experience of love, however impermanent, is worth any price, the bearing of any heartache, heartbreak, and anguish which will follow. However bittersweet the memories, there is always the "sweet," which is the holy grail of living a human life. It is in the nature of humans to anticipate great love, like a morning of "coffee rich / cream thick / bacon becon[ing] from cast iron pan."

"Happiness tiptoes / silent as stars / between us. . . Sew the memory to your soul."

This author exhibits equal parts courage,

boldness, and a refined receptivity to her own sense of how the world is put together—her humanness flows opulently through one poem to the next, as one thread may string a whole Christmas full of popcorn and cranberries.

If you are going to ignore a poetry book this year, don't let it be this one.

From the start, E.J. takes big bites of the apple, and never relinquishes her bold grasp of the big picture. She speaks eloquently of romantic love, but also of the familial love of parents and children and siblings. She notes the anguish of lost love, and not only the loss of a lover. There is the "pale sorrow reserved / for those who die too young," as well as the parching loneliness after widowhood arrives.

These poems celebrate the yearning for love, the intensity of love, the exquisite pain of lost love, and the abiding ravenousness for more. There is almost a rejoicing in the pain of lost love as the emblem or proof of having experienced love—which is the be all, regardless of how it ends.

E.J.'s language of heartbreak is eloquent—"the fallible heart sewn loosely to our sleeve", "& how / a heart breaking / almost / never / makes a sound. . ." And the uppercut: "You promised / growing old was something / we'd do / together. / But still, / you didn't stay."

The emotions accompanying the loss of exquisite love are stunningly recorded, with passages like this:
"We'll be okay. . ."
And "Oh" "My" "God"
which is perhaps,
the only prayer that matters.

E.J.'s directive is to shun false hope, and dig for the real, no matter how it ends.

Remembrance of immense pain from the past is always outweighed by recollection of the good parts. She also reminds us that experience as well as memory is a personal journey—not everything can be shared, or needs to be. But we personally need to

cherish our own priceless memories, even if they are
"folded inside songs, scents / and scars that still ache /
when it rains."

Even when the future assuredly promises
to be total heartbreak, we can't help but "impale
ourselves on / misplaced dreams / and swagger
into love / like sailors / on a three day leave. . ." And
yet, she admonishes to never shy from love — ". . .
I'll remember / my hand against your skin / never
wishing / I'd touched you less." And the immediacy
of the present: *Forgive my cold, cold feet, / smell the
lilacs in my hair, believe / this, my only truth, / I love you
now.*"

E.J. not only encourages the ruthless pursuit of
that which we can't ignore, but celebrates those who,
no matter what, engage in the dance: "I raise my glass
in silent honor / of your grace."

Laced throughout these poems are subtle images
of life and love, which gently advance the ambience
of each poem. But most unmistakably prevalent are
those images of the moon. Quiet, at times elegant,
engaged, and ardent, but at other times alone, distant,
longing, and in most every instance possessing of a
grace which mirrors our complex poetic narrator.

And it is the subtle complexity of E.J.'s work that
is as enticing as first love, and as heartbreakingly
beautiful of what much surely follow.

This is not a poetic work to be taken lightly, for
the exuberance of joy and clarity, and the ache and
agony of the author's lessons from her journey can't
help but rub off and inspire her readers.

There is an abundance here for the taking.

—Tracy Mitchell, poet and trusted friend

No Matter How It Ends

Finalist of The Birdy Poetry Prize—2022
by Meadowlark Press

No Matter How It Ends

poems by

E.J. Rode

Meadowlark Press, LLC
meadowlarkpoetrypress.com
P.O. Box 333, Emporia, KS 66801

No Matter How It Ends

Cover art & design by Tracy Million Simmons
Author photo by E.J. Rode
Interior design by Linzi Garcia

POETRY / Women Authors
POETRY / Subjects & Themes / Love
POETRY / Subjects & Themes / Nature

ISBN: 978-1-956578-30-0
Library of Congress Control Number: 2022949214

For Eric and Lisa

i carry your heart (i carry it in my heart)
e. e. cummings

The Morning After

Love is always a miracle
no matter how it ends

for a time we walk
with the sun on our faces

warmed deeper than our skin
we are new

shocked from complacency
rousted from bitterness

by this unexpected grace
this movable feast

we've forever hungered for
how sweet at last to savor

with no cast shadow
of what will come

no matter how it ends
we begin believing

always awake
praying for a miracle

Table of Contents

ONE

TWO

THREE

FOUR

ONE

Early

It is morning
in mother's kitchen.
Outside
is a dim light-blue sky
full of cloud bellies
that blush persimmon
as the sun pushes high.
Inside
is wood-stove warm
a silver percolator perches
proudly on the countertop
singing the early song
as dark coffee erupts, staccato,
inside the glass lid.
My father morning-stretches into the kitchen,
mother fills his cup
and laughs as he whispers
morning nonsense against her neck.
Our small, safe kitchen
is full of scents,
mother's clean cotton dress
father's spicy after-shave
buttered toast
coffee rich with thick cream
and bacon beckoning
from a cast iron skillet.
Good
morning.

Be Here

Late night
familiar faces
and perfect strangers
softened by smiles.
Happiness tiptoes
silent as stars
between us all.

Be here
now,
hear a friendly voice
memorize a smile.

Tomorrow will come
soon enough.
Don't hurry.
Hold this time
priceless in your hand
your heart your mind.

Sew this memory
to your soul
chances are you'll need it
somewhere
down the road.

Sassafras

During the Ozark chapter
of my childhood
my brother
became enamored
with sassafras tea.

He boiled pot after
pot of his pungent
botanical brew
crafting
his own contentment.

The memory of a scent
is not a scent at all
but a gentle wafting friend
provocateur
of involuntary recall

of how an older brother
smiled, and sometimes
whistled as he stirred his tea
in the blue mug he loved
and how he played

an old forty-five record
by Johnny Cash
The Orange Blossom Special
over and over
and over again

till scent and song
joined into one
entwined with the word
sassafras

and they somehow

became memory's
cornerstone
a path leading me back
to my brother, alive again
stirring his tea.

Last Rites of Winter

I thought of you today with
my feet firmly on the floor, cold
in the pre-light morning of my bedroom.
Today you would have been sixty-five,
if you'd stuck around.

You would have hated it. Citizenship
with seniors is no laughing matter.

Would you have hated it
or are you happier as you are?
Forever a brown-eyed girl
frozen in sepia-tinted memory
recalled with the pale sorrow reserved
for those who die too young.

Would you rather have aged?
To have adapted to wrinkles and discounts,
the mild ache on chilly mornings
time marching across your face
dimming your brown eyes,
leaving you fumbling on the bed table
for your bifocals.

Inside

There must be a thousand ways
to be inside
instead of out.

Inside
can mean so many things
the inside joke
or inside track
the insider's unique knowledge
or going inside
and never looking back.

Outside are birds and blooms
the sunshine day
the mysterious moon
the smiles, the waves, the sound
of someone calling out "Hello,"
the expanse of all the places
one might choose to go.

Inside holds the things
that hold us
in place
the windows, books, photos, walls
that confine, yet comfort
with familiarity's casual grace
as if a house could be a body
and we its heart
cradling sacred secrets
inside.

Old House

When I cross
my kitchen floor, sunlight

slants my path
already headed toward afternoon.

Two bowls nested
in the cupboard kiss

a porcelain heartbeat
rim to rim keeping time

with my moving feet.
It's almost music, almost annoying.

I'd miss it
if it stopped.

Now I'm pouring
cereal into a white bowl and

cutting a banana
in half the way my mother did

near the end
when the whole of anything was

much more than
she could bear.

The upper cupboard
only pretends to close then

comes ajar as
I turn my back, just a crack

revealing everything I'd
washed and blessed and put away.

Moon Dance

My mind is crowded
with planets, stars
and poetry.
The full moon
looms
just days away
tugs
not playfully
at my emotional sea.
Stars shine.
Poetry tumbles
    from the barrel of my pen.
Who wrote that?
I wonder
trying to push the words back in.
Where to start?
Where to end?
I sleep.
I wake
begin again
longing for a lullaby
softer than
my life
louder than
my dreams.

against the wall

it isn't real
not the way we think of real
as something we can catch

between our folding fingers
to turn and test
finding fault

lines that mark old wounds
more or less healed
or mended wrong and left

not real as what
we bring to our lips
questioning the whole

by the part
is it sweet
does it burn the tongue

or leave us wanting
something pure
and less or more than

what we query
with our teeth
biting and swallowing

whole or spitting out
it isn't real like that
it's illusion—a trick

painted on the wall
shadows we almost see
from the corner of our eye

as we turn from memory
to walk toward
or away from what

we cannot touch
avoid the trailing shadows
that stain the walls

with this replica of time
the shutter clicks
a moment caught

the fallible heart sewn loosely
to our sleeve
our hands reaching

Knowing

before
& after
& up &
down
& how we all know
about
what goes around
black & white
lost
& found
pockets
full of posies
then falling down
& how
a heart breaking
(especially on a rainy day)
almost
never
makes a sound
just like
ashes
& ashes
falling down

Fall

You left too soon
you, the one
who was late
for everything.
What made you go?
Never mind.
I know,
I'll never know.

So many years
come
and gone
without you
children grown
grandbabies voting
my heart still trying
to mend
my wrinkles deep
and hair gone gray.

You promised
growing old was something
we'd do
together.
But still,
you didn't stay.

Rain

I.

I can't trust the mystery
of the ringing phone
the way you never know
what's waiting on the other end.
will it be just a hello
a tale told of a banal day
the casual chit-chat
of nothing much to say.
Or will it go
the other way?
The never-saw-that-coming way
that sinks you to your knees.
The way that makes your mind
stop
and sends it grasping for clichés
"that's going to leave a mark. . ."
"this will end in tears. . ."
"this too will pass. . ."
"we'll be okay. . ."
and "Oh" "My" "God"
which is, perhaps,
the only prayer that matters.

II.

I hate the lie
of the sunshine day
the grass
the birds
the tender air
the false belief
that everything will be okay.
Send me dark clouds
send me thunder
louder than the pain
and please, please
send me rain.

Storytime

If words could make wishes come true. . .
      —Jim Croce

if I could wish you
here again
I'd be with you
right now

Sitting next to you
legs curled against your hip
the way I always did
sheltered somehow
halfway in your lap.

I'd never look away
from your face
as if it was the light
and I'd lived in darkness
all my days.

I'd press my face
against your chest
fill my lungs
to the point of exploding
with the scent
of your skin and

beg you to talk and talk and talk
till your voice
was a tattoo on my soul.
Didn't you know
that you were the story
I always wanted to hear?

Tell me again.

What I Remember

Secretly watching
   as my mother stood silent
    in the moon-washed green shadow
   of the avocado tree beside our house.
   the dark air drunk, reeling, from the scent
   of roses and jasmine.

Why was she there
   waiting for the moon, for the clouds?
   In that silent moment
   my mother seemed
   mysterious
   a stranger
   unknown
   a woman alone
   in her own night garden.

I remember the taste
   of childhood's breath
   rushing through me
   shared in words and sighs
   splinters of sound
   half heard words
   whispered dreams
   small, sweet secrets
   and time
   rushing past
   lost days
   a mystery
   I'll never get back.

Brave Again

Tomorrow
I will be brave again.
My tears
will have dried by then.
I will hold my head high,
and give everyone smiles
for miles.

All they will see
is my everyday face,
not the aching
empty place.

No one will know that
last night I cried
at a graveside.

Light

Forgive yourself
for everything
large and small, all
the books you never read,
temper you lost
people you couldn't love back
bad television you watched
walks you took while
duty stood three feet away
and glared.
Forgive the times you didn't dare
and the times you didn't care
and didn't try.
Forgive the past you cannot change.
The only absolution that matters
is the one you make.
Pour the holy water
over your own bowed head.
It's penance enough
and more.
Carry what you must,
the memory of it all
folded inside songs, scents
and scars that still ache
when it rains.
Pull the nails you
hammered into your own soft hands.
Leave behind the dead things
that refuse the grave.
Finally know
that you cannot stay.
Travel light.

TWO

Reckless

Infatuation comes too easy
        and reality too often late
we stumble over words
impale ourselves on
        misplaced dreams
and swagger into love
        like sailors
        on three-day leave
far from the familiar
half drunk and drooling
        prepared for nothing
hopes high
        smiles unstoppable.

best regards

For e.e. cummings

my dear old ampersand
i'm writing poetry   again
a tricky task for   as you know

                        i watch television   &
when someone says dylan, i
always think of bob but i try
to put my distractions aside

        & focus   on the task at hand
        & what   i mean to say

        you know what I mean ampersand

you've always understood that
        root & tree are not
meant to be apart   you & i
make sense
                        more sense than
parens
                or tildes or commas
                        what good are symbols
& all that they enjoin
if   we speak only in code

with proper punctuation

                ampersand it is you   who makes the moon

                                make sense

Sunset

When I am an older old
than I am now
I will remember walking
the easy swing of it
step after step
without a thought
my faithful body moving
while I remain lost in how
changing light burnishes
the brick wall to precious metal
gilds the edges
of an overblown rose
and how the crows fly
like dark glyphs against
the fading light
unlikely as paper cut-outs
taking flight.

I'll remember
every evening walk
without regret
the same way I'll remember
my hand against your skin
never wishing
I'd touched you less.

Unless

Don't pull the curtain.
Not tonight. The moon
and I will watch you fall
into your easy sleep.

Beneath the crust of white
the frozen ground burns with cold
and waits slumbering in the flames.
The snow is only smoke.

Wind moans through bare
branch trees and flees
through drifts of winter
white. Beyond the crack
of ice, spring slips in

on pussy-willow feet
daily closer, carrying
the industry of nesting birds,
rebirth of blooms
and weighted limbs of ripening.

I cannot stand in only
one season at a time. Each
day holds the seeds of
what will come and the smoldering
ashes of what has passed.

We balance on the fulcrum
of now and then; a crone
with a child's smile, a
boy with the weary eyes
of a prophet,

and lift our faces to the wind.

Forgive my cold, cold feet,
smell the lilacs in my hair, believe
this, my only truth,
I love you now.

Sequel to Yesterday

It is early morning.
We are in bed
still.

On the radio
a man reads a poem.
We listen
grateful for a reason
not to rise.
It ends and from across
the bed my love says
"Don't you wish
we could live inside the poem
not get up
not go?"

In the silence after
I remember falling
and how dear the cost to rise.

Beneath the blanket
our hands touch
and I wish with him.

Dancing at O'Neill's

I love the girls who dance alone
the plain ones   and those broad of hip
the way they sway   shift their weight
side to side   slide   rest
one beat softening   into the next
heads down   absorbed

and the women   the older ones
who rise on spider veins and aching feet
moving   moved by music
shaking rounded breasts
and bellies soft
with children borne decades past
eyes closed   old feet remembering
another life   how it moved   how they learned
these steps

what moves in you   moves   in me
still and watching   this
   your solitary beauty that
(for once) does not care   who looks   what shows
there is no right way to dance   only
dim light   the margin of the floor   where
couples do not tread   music   so loud
that sound becomes   a disguise

    the signs on the walls
paint your curved lips   slender necks   strong backs
      with stained glass shades of neon
gilding your unexpected perfection

I raise my glass   in silent honor
of your grace

Linger

rain swept through
last night
while I slept

left a lingering
wet kiss
on the lawn

along with a clean
wafting scent
like a sometimes lover
gone before dawn.

Moonshine

Beyond the clouds
in the space
I cannot see

the full moon still shines

faithful to her task
she transforms the clouds
to conduit

sending diffused light

to paint the snow
beneath my feet
to neon white.

The cloud-light above
and the alchemical-white below
call out, each to the other

like lovers a universe apart

speaking a language
that joins light to light
and soaks a waiting earth

The Equation
(A Poem in Parenthesis)

Happiness equals what we have divided by what we expect.
    —Edward Edinger

It goes like this:
Your reality
(crow's feet, extra pounds
that mock your jeans, crabgrass,
flat-tire, degree you never
got, job you did, trip to Paris
you've been saving for forever,
novel buried in the bottom drawer,
endless lists of un-met shoulds,
friends who stayed, dreams that
didn't, the exuberant everyday blaze
of watercolor sunrise that makes you
think—in spite of everything—God
is not indifferent after all, red wine, hand-
holding, good music, poetry &
thank God the kids are
okay) Reality,

Divided by:
(of course there's a divided by, that wet-
dream of sadistic elementary teachers
determined to impart that
anything that can be joined, added to,
multiplied, achieved or almost
achieved can be) Divided by,

Your expectations:
(What did you expect? A question
always posed in a voice that dares
an answer, and what answer—however

true—doesn't reek of the fool, your own
adolescent dreams dressed up in
business clothes and pushed upon a
stage to mumble secret wishes
to bored strangers in tight shoes. Who could
say the truth? You expected more than
what and how and who you are.)
You expected to shine.

Equals:
(Realize this word is
a lie. There is no equality. One breast
is always a bit bigger, one nostril a bit higher
one twin faster. Someone is smarter, prettier,
luckier and sometimes
that someone is you.
Pray the scale tips towards
grace
and know things are only equal
in algebra and even then, it isn't even)
Equals

Your happiness.
(There's logic here—logic that espouses
what you expected and what came next
can be divided by better
or worse and ignores the glaring
possibility that what you
settled for—imperfect house,
spouse in need of repairs,
job your father said you were better than,
burnt toast, drooling dog, practical car—
wasn't settling after all.
The course you set
and tumbled from a thousand times
taught you that the weeds growing in the ditch
you landed in were sweeter than

the flowers you planned to plant
in your perfect life—which you still might find
when you have time
but you'd hate to leave behind
what just might be)
Your happiness.

When We Speak of Motion

From the moment we arrive we are
   on our way somewhere
else, somewhere
   not here, some
   place where we might find
   the illusive, nameless, something
   we can't stop missing.

Perhaps the ocean lives in us
contained but always churned
   by storms, tides, endless waves
   eternally seeking a shore
   that banished us long ago.

Maybe it's the moon that moves us
waxing, waning
   traveling sky's end to
   sky's end, affixed to this
   magnet, this earth, yet wanting
   more than orbit.

We speak of what moves us,
   art, music, dance
   flickering lines of words
   on paper
   the gentle light
   of autumn.

I am here

                 next to you.
Your long thigh pressed to mine.
Your hand, still warm from your coffee cup,
                 curves to the curve

of my heart. I am held
in place, anchored
by what set me free,
but I still feel

        the pull of the moon.

Concession

If you speak softly
I will lean in
and listen harder.

If you bring me flowers
I will hope that "sorry"
means sorrow.

If you talk about tomorrow
I will trust that we are safe
for today.

If you hold my hand
I will feel
your heart.

If you give to me
I will give
too.

If you love me
I will love you back.

The Rug

there are not words
not enough
not the right ones
to help us
escape
from this place
we never intended to be

the world is empty
as a pocket
the day before
the payday
that never comes

someone pulled the rug
the rug we never looked at
because
it was just a rug
a taken-for-granted
rug
that was just
there
almost invisible
until it was gone

then the absence
was a chasm
empty except
for the echo

and the floor
was cold
and so very hard

Repair

an interesting word
as if a pair
that was a pair
but isn't
could be re-paired
again
it rhymes with
despair
to de-pair
a pair
then give them
(as a consolation prize)
The sibilance of an S
give them sorrow
sadness, sacrifice
scars and sudden
surrender
their silent
solo hearts
finally certain
there is no repair

Saint Anthony's Mother

I wish my heart was light
  as a gossamer wing
  caged within my chest

And not this jagged
  shard of ice
  that aches with every breath

August Morning

I heard the geese this morning,
the wild ones
winging overhead.
Their voices woke me
where I lay
warm and lazy on my bed.
And I thought
it's only August
surely summer is not past.
The only answer was their echo
moving south
fading fast.

I have cunning devices
man-made ways
to portion out my life
into
minutes
hours
days.
Theirs is wisdom
born of being
exactly as they're made.
That wisdom lends them motion
while I in stillness
wonder
why I stay.

Tonight

I will tell the moon
all the things
I cannot say
to you.

#7

Close the door
softly
and slow.
Close it tight.
I don't want
even the memory
of the light
you take
when you go.

~~~

This is
the most truth
I can tell you:
I hate you
almost as much
as I love you.
Or the other way around.

~~~

What the thunder said

—T. S. Eliot, The Wasteland

after the storm
and the screaming
accusations
anger threats and tears
         so many tears

the air goes still
heavy as a shroud
sorrow stays silent
         but so very loud

shock sets in
fear whispers in the corner
unasked questions
         sit in every chair

what now
where do we go
         from here

the answer doesn't answer
the thunder holds its tongue
         the waiting has begun

waiting to stop waiting
waiting to move on
waiting to know while
         treading water in the unknown

and finally
thunder's answer comes
         "now live with what you've done"

THREE

Victory

A certain joy comes along
with giving up.

Muscles melt from stone,
to flesh again.

Knuckles surrender the white-hot war
of holding on.

Stiff at first
hands slowly remember how,

to unfurl, like sparrow wings
before fall or flight.

Allow gravity its win,
as falling begins.

Mending

choose the sharpest needle
pierce the fabric nearest the thread
pull
despite the resistance

against the unraveling of what
was sewn fine and true
do not relent

had you seen the future
perhaps you would have chosen
weaker thread
looser stitches

never mind, make another
brutal stab
feel the surrender
of faithful thread

examine those
bloodless wounds
left behind

only empty holes remain
peel asunder
what was joined

it is done
your heart is off your sleeve
a limp scrap

scarred by needle bites
it barely fills your hand
and what to do with it
now

The Deep Dark Calendar
of the Soul

January snakes its way inside
just past midnight, pauses long enough
to snag its worn out skin
on our threshold, then moves along.
    A paper-thin carcass we'll return to again and again.

February doesn't like it here,
doesn't plan to stay, allows us only
twenty-eight days
and the beating heart at its center.
    Full of hope and illusion.

March does exactly that;
stomps its way across a month full
of temper tantrums and bitter winds
or flirts with tender breezes
    then leaves us shivering in the cold.

April is an indecisive lover
overrun with seduction, tears and broken promises.
She weeps while picking our pockets
plants our yards with tender blooms
    then burns them up with blizzards.

May is the sly one, opening the door with a wink
Then it's Maybe there will be sunshine
Maybe not. Maybe a fine day
or a tempest in your favorite teapot.
    It's only here to break your heart.

June is a nestled, Goldilocks dream
of everything just right. Nothing too skimpy
and nothing too much. Luxuriate

in these too-brief days.
    Good things rarely last.

July and August show up holding hands,
lazy overheated twins sweating indifference.
The garden is full of weeds. The lawn wants mowing
and fireworks only serve to scare the dog.
    Those twins always stay too long.

September strolls in on a tightrope.
Watch as your green feast of shade shifts
to a golden canopy, then drifts downward
becomes a crackling carpet of blazing autumn
    that breaks beneath your feet.

October is the alley cat
you never quite see
only feel, tingling
at the back of your neck.
    A mystery always ready to pounce.

November glides in
silent as an owl seeking prey.
Its glowing, knowing eyes
send a shiver down your soul.
    Things are about to go deep.

December flings the door wide
and strides inside; too loud, too
bright, too much force-fed joy
then leaves us empty.
    Three more months of winter.

And the world keeps going around.

My Stars

My true north has morphed
somehow
into a wandering star.
Believe me when I say
I'm happy
for those of you who know
exactly where you are

you who know the number
of steps from here to home
trust the key
will always fit the lock

I used to be
a part of your tribe.

When I wasn't looking
my north star came undone
unmoored
unreliable
unprepared.

It's not itself at all.

Every time I think
I've found my way
mapped my path
packed my bags
said my fare-thee-wells

that old star shifts.
Plans come apart.
I don't know
the way home

and I can barely
hear my heart.

Who fixes stars?
Who brings them back
when the wandering starts?

Can we nail them
to the sky
cage them
make them simply
abide?

Is this why
stars die
why they fall
streaking across the sky

carrying the weight
of our whispered wishes
heavy as darkness
while they burn
the last of their light?

Maybe stars grow weary
and wish for home.

Predictability
can feel so very nice
but heaven knows
the price.

Wild Horses

Does the world look tattered
because parts of me
have shattered?

Does the sky hang lower
clouds frowning
because
all the words I can't say
are painted gray?

Does the earth skitter
sideways
all logic abandoned
because my thoughts
are wild horses
chasing thunder down a canyon?

I cannot catch them.

Does my dog bark at nothing
because she gathers
all the words
I am not strong enough
to speak
and barks them to the sky
so they can breathe?

White Shelf

They've painted the house we used to live in,
a dark blue-gray that makes it sit heavy on the lot.
In the front yard, the aspen tree we planted still thrives
though the Russian sage and the iris have died.

The green pot we bought together one random weekend
years past, crouches in the tall grass.
In the backyard, the roses, grown tall, bend softly
beneath the weight of their blooms.
The white shelf I nailed to the fence—that place
to set my wine glass and your beer, near to hand,
waits faithfully, not knowing;
we will not be together there again
will not share the silly toast
the tender kiss of glasses rim to rim
as the sun slides down the cloud strewn sky.

In the gloaming, I trespass while the owners are away,
breathe the scent of who we used to be,
recall the life we squandered
indifferent to the fragile beauty of an ordinary day.

If I soften my gaze, ignore the new paint,
take in only the shape of the house, the familiar
objects we left behind, the scent of roses,
for a moment, I almost believe I could walk to the door
open it
and step back into love.

Breaking

The evening news
casts a shadow across

Over and over again I find
myself lost

Nightmare the debt too large
to be paid

Nightmare lives lost to
the games that are played

Nightmare the spinning words
that spew nonstop

That stink of sulfur and lava
death and rot

I pour the wine and close
my eyes

Even the truth has learned
how to lie

A Tale

It was the best of times.
People were home
proud owners of long overdue
freedom.
Parents were ever available
to children accustomed
to parenting themselves.

They parked their cars
took their confused dogs
for long walks
cracked open dusty books
long forgotten
slowed down long enough
to look their stranger/spouses
eye to eye.

It was the worst of times.
Death had written their address
or at least
they feared he had.
Poverty lurked in their forsythia bushes
peered in their windows
leered at their door.
Their parents called
in tears
to share their fears
and beg them to stay home
wear a mask
stay six feet past
anyone
everyone
don't even look in mirrors
too long.

Their jobs didn't call
and didn't call
and the not-calls
rang so loud
the house shook.

In the evening
when the light seeped out
and the dust stood still
they sat quietly
alone
together
and whispered every fear
barely louder than a breath
unsure if it was prayer
or simply conversation
held hands
afraid to use the word
"when"
and all the words
that might come after.

Listing

i

sometimes i think
i'd like to set my house
aflame
watch, dance & weep
while it burns

technology first
computer, phone, tablet
television, remote
let the circuits sizzle
while my scorched secrets
vanish

goodbye dog-eared books
ill-advised diaries
the fragile memorabilia
of the life i thought i'd lived

i'd stay to the end
waiting till even my skin
absorbed the pungent smell
that might mean
i've gone to hell

ii

sometimes i think
i'd like to move
to england
or maybe seattle
& live on a boat

let the ocean rock me
sing the lullaby

of lapping waves
let salt air wash
the scent
of yesterday's sins
off my skin

iii

sometimes i think
i'll change my name
let the under-appreciated alchemy
of letters
weave a brand-new me
with a brand-new smile
new purpose
new dreams
same old scars

no matter where you go
there you are

iiii

sometimes i think
i think too much
go far too far
& lose my way

the saints never come
to save me
the angels
fold their wings
& maybe take a nap

i'd give everything I own
if only heaven
would sell me a map

In the Details

God and the devil both
reside inside the details.
The miracle of a feather
defines an angel's wing
and found, though small
can become a sign
to point a pilgrim's path.

And what of the other face,
the shifting cunning foe?
What marks the trail he takes?
what helps us track and slay
the beast that threatens
our fragile peace?

The bond between what we find
and what we seek is stronger
than the tide
and will carry us down paths
our torches cannot light
will twist us
until our world
becomes a maze.

In the end
the monster that we will find
often turns out to be
the monster that we made.

Hush

inside the silent houses
someone waits
for coffee to brew
hopes
the children sleep
a little longer
prays for more minutes
of solitude

down the street
a pair of lovers
wake
look across the sheets
to that same familiar face
grown more
essential
more dear
year by year
they
touch
old hand to old hand
whisper "hello"
rise slow
shuffle into morning
knowing their days
dwindle
refuse to number
even one
silently scold the clock for ticking

hush

Sugarplums Gone Mad

At 2 a.m.
all the things
I do not know
and cannot decide
dance above my head
like sugarplums gone mad
while the ghosts
of follies past
perch on the edge
of my bed
crowding my feet
and sneering their
all-knowing sneer.

I hear the double-dog-dare
they never bother to speak.

All the rest of me
is middle
neither here
nor there.
Hours tick past.
The steady momentum of life
waits
for me
to decide.

Sleepwalking

There are days when I almost forget,
when I am made of muscle, bone
and gristle
a thumping heart
and blood
rushing, rushing, rushing.

I endure my monotone days.

Then
my half-forgotten soul
finds me again.
I feel it
warm as the hand
of a friend
upon my shoulder.
Suddenly, the cup I hold that
a second past was just
another weight to carry—becomes
a red cup with the rising vapor of
sweet cream and coffee teasing
my nose.

Above me the moon
swims in dark blue
though the east is
ripening to gold. Soon
sun and moon will share
the still, wide sky.

The apricot
light of morning will lap against
the moon's far shore
and I will
turn my face toward heaven, toward
grace, toward all the miracles I
forgot to look at yesterday.

Moon-while

A half-moon hangs
      like a broken bulb
indifferent to
the wind-ruffled boughs
writhing
      so far below.

The gate
not properly latched
screeches
wood against wood
then slaps
      a brutal confrontation
      as if a grudge, long held
      has finally combusted.

Treetop high
small leaves
shimmy
as the midnight tempest
fingers its way
along
the song of solstice.

The stars
and I
      wide awake
      bemused and grateful
bear witness.

Friday Nights

There's something
in a Friday night
that's lonelier
than other nights.

Maybe, deep down
we believe
Friday night
was made for lovers.

We feel we've failed

when we sit alone,
hands un-held,
mouths un-kissed,
sweet words unspoken,

trapped forever
behind someone's lips,
laughter that never
touches the air,

loving gazes doomed
to become vacant stares,
hearts that beat
in silent rooms

unheard, unfelt, untouched,
unseen except
by the occasional
Friday night moon.

Danger

the sky is crowded
clogged
with clouds

i fear the moon
is about
to drown

all i do is sit
and stare
at everything that isn't there

who am i
to save the moon
an old dreamer alone

in an empty room

Me & the Dog

I'm drinking alone
with my dog
writing the poems
that refuse to write themselves.

It may sound like lonely times
but my eyes are open wide.
Dreams surround me
like broken wings

while I write the poems
of broken things.
And my dog, she doesn't judge
just lets me do what I am here to do

and never turns her face away
stands watch with me
while the night
crawls towards day.

Yearling

I didn't fall ill
nor drown
in depression's dark waters.
I did not carry fear
like a cancer in my gut
till it ate me up.
I didn't let inconvenience
turn me small and mean
though there were dark days
when every bad thing
called my name.

Instead
I talked to God
and my dog
learned to hear
my ancestors whisper
and sometimes curse
"We survived worse
  so, dammit, fight
  for your flawed
  but precious life."

About a Bird

I tried to write a poem
about a robin
about the blood-orange fruit
of its feathered chest
and how looking at it
gave my eyes a rest after
winter's long and weary march.

But in the end
nothing came of it
the poem, and its false start.
It seems I can only write of hearts
of their beating and bleeding
their falling and the secrets they keep,

but mostly, of bruised, abandoned
or broken hearts
and their broken parts.
I paste these words onto pages,
like assemblage, like a
broken form of art.

Which brings me back
to the robin
who watches me with
unwavering eyes, wary but
abiding in spite.
For the first time
I wonder at his heart
beneath his fiery feathers
a small, beating thing
so very far
from his wings.

FOUR

Welcome

The scent of tangerines
        washes my kitchen.
A gentle curve of fallen peel
        graces the countertop
with an unexpected still life.

I bite into membrane
        feel my mouth flood
        cool juice
        fiber that held
        the whole together
swallow joy.

It's been so long
        since I saw myself.

Yarding

There are more weeds
than marigolds
no matter how hard I try
and even grass
        is in short supply.

The morning glories
I've been watering
might be bindweeds
only time will tell
        so watering proceeds.

At Yarding 101 it seems
I'm a proper failure.
I'd live on a houseboat,
yard free, if I wasn't
        even worse as a sailor.

But when the sun surrenders
the moon slow-climbs
the sky
and backyard solar lights
flare on laying claim
        to the night

cast their shadows wide
soften weeds to just
another shade of green.
My sore back
sighs into a seasonal chair
and suddenly
        I don't care.

The maybe bindweed
looks fine on that trellis
and it doesn't matter

if no one ever
looks at my yard
          and feels jealous.

I can sit here, content,
in this kindly
flaw-hiding glow
and humbly thank God
          that it's too dark to mow.

True Nature

Never expect the sun
to explain the nature
of the night.

He slides away before
darkness opens the door
onto a gallery of stars,

before the moon claims
her throne and casts
enchantment's light

painting our daylight world
in shadow's sly hue.
We swallow illusions whole, while

our mad, melancholy queen
watches wide-eyed and feral
waxing fat and glowing

on a diet of dreams
waning to brittle bones
when reality fills her bowl.

Wait out the night.

Save your love
for someone
kinder than the moon.

Things Undone

There are things I do poorly
yet love so well.
Punctuation comes to mind,
poetry, the piano and prayer.
My best intentions wilt in the heat
of rules.

Some say it is the flesh that is weak,
but my flesh is lively, and rarely still.
it sweeps my spirit along in its tide,
and when the tide recedes
I am left,
less than my dreams
and yet,
and yet.

It is always love in some form
great or small, that catches me up
and carries me along
spinning
undone by a name, a song, a nuance
a burning need.

Of my failings I can only tell
I've fallen short
but loved so well.

Some Days

I want to spray-paint hope
large
across my heart
bright and dripping color
like a rainbow
over-full of everything good.

I want to pour mercy
around my feet
watch it puddle
and soak in
like holy water
on long-parched ground.

I want
green things
conceived in hope
to sprout from mercy
tiny shoots
of tenderness
growing strong
against the odds.

For what is hope
but love, a dream
made tangible?

And what is mercy
but everything
we always knew
we didn't deserve
and couldn't earn
that finds us anyway
exactly
where we are?

Routine

the omnipotent they
say
I need a routine
to ground me
sew me safe
to this unstable world
and guide me through
the current inconvenience

they say
If I craft a routine
carve it
carefully
claim it
as my own
I'll be better

and I wonder
better than what?
and does no routine
render me
less better
than those who
rise consistently
consume food
with bovine predictability
and remember
where they left their keys?

the omnipotent they
smile so gratefully
upon those
who practice routine
they will probably

report me
to the authorities
(whoever they may be)

I'd flee
but I can't find my keys

Inexplicable

I am about to put my hands
into this poem
elbow deep in what it means
to poet. To write. To be
one who lives behind closed doors and
shuttered smiles. I want to unleash
private truth upon this public page.

In my youth I thought all poets were
young, slender, ethereal
a mystery clothed in long
dark hair and a midnight soul.

I am none of that. Not now. Not ever.
Youth flew the coop while I was too busy
to even wave goodbye. Long hair is tedious
and clogs the drains. My soul is still
a rebel-child
refusing every offered niche.

I will tell you this—
untamed words can rage
loud as any earthquake,
as soul-killing as a prison term
dangerous as a sea storm
that does not know
how to stop.
Words can toss you in the tempest
leave you half-drowned on some wretched beach
where no one knows your name and there are no
umbrella drinks.
You will thank them later.

I would explain,

but it's like trying to explain the moon.
There are so many ways to do it.
All of them are lies and all of them are true.
The moon is always too much, and never enough.

It's like that.

For Dreams

Some days
I yearn for summer's
warm kiss
for endless sunsets
floating cotton clothing
that never demands layers
days that beg for lemonade
floppy hats
the summer-scent
of sunburn cream
homegrown tomatoes
wide open roads
calling my name.

But winter
is good for dreams
the early dark
soundless snow
that haunts my soul
the cold, illusive moon
slipping in and out of clouds
like a sly celestial spy
reminding us
not everything
is what it seems. Yes
winter is made for dreams
and wishes
cast in the dark
like seeds
that float to frozen ground
on winter's breeze
land softly
and burrow deep.

Winter has promises to keep.
They grow
while we sleep.

Cartography

Lie down
windows open wide.

Listen to the cicadas
saw the midnight sky.

Let the stars
eavesdrop on your prayers.

Dream the dreams
of old souls.

Let moonlight
soft as milk

be the blanket
that comforts your bones.

Trace the lines
across your face and know

this is the only map you need
to lead you home.

In Between

local labyrinth overlooked
between churchyard
and lake

calls my name

geese honk
crows caw
trees sentinel

breath cascades
lungs draw deep
tears dry

thoughts calm
steps slow
mindfully

going
nowhere
almost as if

being alive
is the prayer
every step

an answer

Balloons Instead

In a week or so
when I am old
I plan to wear
red shoes
and carry a cloud
of yellow balloons
above my head.
If it rains
and some need umbrellas
I'll have my balloons
instead.
Yellow balloons to float above me
like my own personal sun
red shoes flash below me
in case I want
to run
and in between
just old wrinkled me
singing to myself
and my pet tambourine.

Flying Things

Pelicans surf my sky
they swoop and turn
churning the blue
with broad white wings

I follow them with my eyes
feel mild envy
for their avian life
no jobs
no masks
no bills to pay
if times are hard
just fly away

but what do I know
of pelican sorrow

it's easy to judge
from the outside in
easy to pretend
to know a pelican

in truth
my ignorance is deep
just as theirs is
of me

i know the shape of them
the way they sweep the sky
their silent swimming dignity

from the outside looking in
i see feathers and beaks
rarely feet or where they stand

beyond that
i find
conjecture and contradiction
a puzzling mystery
exactly as you see
looking at me

Practice

Falling isn't as easy
as one might think,
though in childhood
it was a daily thing.
We bounced and rose,
and ran again, but now
we've forgotten how.
Try falling. Go ahead.
Toss yourself down the stairs
or trip on air
or the corner of the rug
pretend the edge came up
and fling yourself into a fall.

See, not as easy as one might think.
And then there is the other fall.

Practice.
Start small, with words, perhaps.
Find a few and hold them, silent,
swirl them across your tongue
then whisper into empty rooms
Adriatic Sea, jungle gym.
Words are easy to love.
That's practice number one.

Inanimate things, or even
the idea of them, are next
Fall for a pair of shoes,
a rusty door, a railroad spike
you might arrange
artfully
somewhere outside with
something flowery vining
just so beside.

Then food.
The perfect BLT
or a slice of chocolate cake
salivate, just picturing that
first bite, perfection blooming
inside your mouth. Just you
and this tasty bit of bliss.

You're getting the hang of it.

Living things are next.
Harder, so start small.
Puppies perhaps.
Hold them to your face.
the puppy smell, the wiggling,
squirming, happy life of them
hemmed in by velvet fur, the
soulful eyes, and busy tongue
hell bent on licking you.
Puppies know all about
how to fall in love.

See how well you've done.
Brace yourself.

Start with someone perfect-ish
since people are so hard.
A celebrity is good, someone you'll never
meet, or smell, or catch in bad grammar
political views you can't possible support,
or eye rolling while you
pour out your heart.

Take as long as you need
to practice there, safe
and once removed.

Real people are next, the sort
who might sit beside you on a bus
or move in next-door and knock
to say hello or ask when trash day comes.
People who may have hair awry
or pants you can't abide, or might be
just fine, except
they don't match the picture in your mind
but there they stand, vulnerable
as imperfect as you
and you wonder
if you've practiced enough.
Falling can be so very tough.

Advice to My Invisible Self

Think less; pray more.
Never argue with those who don't understand.
Don't try so hard.

Laugh more; pray less.
Remind yourself to remember.
Take the risk; it might be your last chance.

Even when someone is watching,
go ahead and dance.

Always buy the good coffee,
good wine, fresh flowers, best chocolate,
and anything your mother ever said
you couldn't afford.

Let people mock the mid-west.
Hope they're always flying over
and never, ever land.

Make a fool of yourself now and then,
but only when it's worth it.

Tell your mind to hush,
and listen to your heart.

Write the poems
you fear no one else will like,

Shred your bank statements;
re-read your old love letters.

Let the wind comb your hair.
Notice the little things.

Keep your heart on your sleeve,
it's happiest there.

Love people,
even when you don't.

About the Author

E.J. has spent most of her life choosing the roads less traveled. She finds joy, sorrow, and, frequently, wisdom in almost everyone she meets. Her work resonates because it is reflective of how much we are alike, even when we differ. Although she has tried her hand at many forms of writing, from fiction and newspaper columns to essays, she always returns to poetry, her first love.

E.J.'s poetry has appeared in *Third Wednesday, The Josephine Quarterly, And/Both Magazine, Zephyr Press,* and *Colorado Living*.

Publication Credits

"Two Lane" - *Third Wednesday* (Summer 2012)

"Dancing At O'Niell's" - *Zephyr*

"Old House" - *The Josephine Quarterly* (Summer 2014)

"Once Full" - *Colorado Life Magazine* (September/ October 2018)

Untitled poem - *And Both Magazine* (September 2019)

"A Tale" - *And Both Magazine* (December 2020)

Acknowledgments

To Wes Hempel who was the first person to read my poetry and cheer me on. There aren't enough words to thank you for five decades of friendship, support and talking me down from one ledge after another. Thank you for making sure a part of me will always be the girl in the white dress.

To my friends and teachers in the Florence Critique Group, you taught me more than you realize. Special thanks to Vaughn Neeld, my friend and mentor and to Marcel Duclos the bearer of light and wisdom.

To Tracy Mitchell, without you this book would still be a lazy dream gathering dust in a dim corner. A favor, so freely given, is not a small thing. Your time, talent, wit, intellect and generosity are gifts for which I will be forever grateful.

Lastly, to Baxter Black, Cowboy Poet, philosopher and best boss ever, who didn't just support and encourage me to keep writing, he insisted I do so. He taught me much and inspired me even more. Happy trails my friend.

Meadowlark POETRY

Books are a way to explore, connect, and discover. Poetry incites us to observe and think in new ways, bridging our understanding of the world with our artistic need to interact with, shape, and share it with others.

Publishing poetry is our way of saying—

We love these words,
we want to preserve them,
we want to play a role in sharing them
with the world.

Follow Meadowlark Press on
Facebook & Instagram

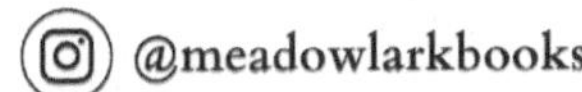

facebook.com/ReadAMeadowlarkBook

@meadowlarkbooks

Birdy Poetry Prize Finalists

2021
Lilac and Sawdust
Kenneth Pobo

"The two men at the center of this book (Jerry and Jeff) are both extraordinary and ordinary, and the poems chart their lives carefully, in great detail, with a loving gaze. The books lets us get to know them, as if they are dear friends, and the writing sparkles, written by someone with clear eyes, clear head, and a clear heart. This book will endear you to it too."
> –Kevin Rabas, Poet Laureate of Kansas, 2017-2019, *More Than Words*

2020
Kansas Poems
Brian Daldorph

"*Kansas Poems* is a poetry of place and microhistory, which nonetheless transcends the people and events it tells about. . . And while I've never been to Kansas, I now feel that I might have—or at least that there is a Kansas of my mind, a place of lakes and fireflies and small lives."
> —Laura Chalar, *Unlearning and Midnight at the Law Firm (Stories)*

Ruth Maus

2019
Valentine
Ruth Maus

"Wry and rue—it sounds like the recipe for a craft cocktail. But those are really the main ingrediients in Ruth Mau's sly, wise, and expansive book. . . Most of her poems are short—and a lot bigger than they seem, poems marked by gallows, humor, and a poker face, and with just a twitch of a tell that reveals how much lies beneath their surface.."
> —Michael Gorra, *Portrait of a Novel: Henry and James and the making of an American Masterpiece*

Meadowlark Press created The Birdy Poetry Prize to celebrate the voices of our era. Cash prize, publication, and 50 copies awarded annually.

Accepting Entries: September 1 - December 1

Entry Fee: $25

Prize: $1,000 cash, publication by Meadowlark Press, 50 copies of the completed book

All entries will be considered for standard Meadowlark publishing contract offers, as well.

Full-length poetry manuscripts (55 page minimum) will be considered. Poems may be previously published in journals and/or anthologies, but not in full-length single-author volumes. Poets are eligible to enter, regardless of publishing history.

See birdypoetryprize.com for complete submission guidelines. Also visit us at meadowlarkbookstore.com